you ARE INCREDIBLE just as you are

HOW TO EMBRACE YOUR PERFECTLY IMPERFECT self

emily coxhead

Vermilion
LONDON

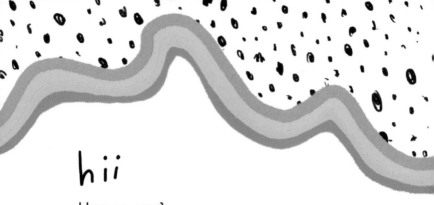

hii

How are you?

I really hope you're doing okay and if things aren't so sparkly at the moment, I hope this book can be a reminder that it's okay not to always be okay, in fact it's pretty important (we are human after all). It's no secret that the world around us is an ever-increasingly weird place that can massively affect us day to day and through the choices we make. This book won't give you all the answers or set you on exactly the right path but I hope it will give you the chance to make some of the right or wrong decisions and figure out what makes you, you, along the way. See, the best thing about this funny old life is that there is nobody else quite like you. There will be people who are similar to you or like the same things as you but there will always be something about you that sets you apart from everyone else. That might sound pretty terrifying but trust me once you realise it, it's such an amazing thing and can be a real weight lifted,

especially when you feel like you're constantly trying to fit into the norm or mold yourself into something or somebody you're not. It feels a little bit ridiculous that I'm dishing out all of the thoughts and advice in this book because I absolutely don't have it all together. In fact, I feel the complete opposite most of the time, but I want this book to be a collection of things I'm figuring out myself alongside a bunch of honest thoughts and scribbles. So here's hoping you or someone you know finds some comfort and happiness in yourself, knowing that we're all making this up as we go... you're doing a pretty great job!

KEEP SMILING,
emily x

getting to know yourself

eep!

ABOUT ME

I'm Emily, I'm the creator of this book and something called _The Happy Newspaper._ I'm a designer, illustrator, author kinda person but also a tea drinker, photographer, greeting card/product designer, cookie maker, night owl, over-thinker, Aquarius, curly-haired kinda person.

ABOUT you

Who am I?

Bit of an intense exercise to start off – you don't need to do this straight away, you can always come back to it. Write five things below that make you, you. Think about five things you like about yourself and think about what other people like about you too:

mine: smiley (most of the time), empathetic, creative, say it how it is (not always a good thing, oops), good cup of tea maker (if I do say so myself)

1.

2.

3.

4.

5.

what is your ~~WEAKNESS~~ SUPER POWER...

MINE:
BEING 'too SENSITIVE'
rolls eyes

I've been told constantly throughout my life that I'm too sensitive, which I thought was a real problem for a long time. I found out about this thing called 'The Highly Sensitive Person', which sounds a bit silly, but when I read up on it and started to understand it more, I realised it's exactly me. I get overwhelmed pretty easily at times, I'm bothered by noises that are too loud or places that are too busy and I feel immense empathy towards people and situations, which is part of the reason I can't always watch the news (but we'll come to that later). I struggle if I'm given too many things to do at once and I know I'm going to have to let people down. There's A LOT to it and I wouldn't say it is always accurate for me, but a huge amount of it is, and since I've realised all of this it makes so much sense to my life. I've grown to love it in recent years; it can be a real weight to carry around at times, but I wouldn't be me without it.

tell me yours...

What is your weakness and how can it be used in a positive way? Think about the things that play on your mind.

DON'T

TO BE

WE'RE ALL totally &

STRIVE

PERFECT

UTTERLY IMPERFECT

BEING

you

you are
super duper

There is nobody else that compares to you. You acquire stuff over the years and you probably long for stuff, materialistic stuff, because that's how the world often makes us feel. But, aside from the new dress, next holiday or number of likes on social media, think about the person without all of that... that's the real, living, messy human being that you are (meant in the best possible way, of course!).

Don't get me wrong; sometimes that holiday or community on Instagram etc. may genuinely help you realise what you need or don't need. This extra stuff might help you find a passion you didn't realise you had or take you on a journey you never expected and meet people you didn't know existed. Of course, this is what life is all about – our experiences, friends, family and jobs all help shape who we become as we grow and are super-important, but try not to lose who you are when you're just being you without all of that stuff.

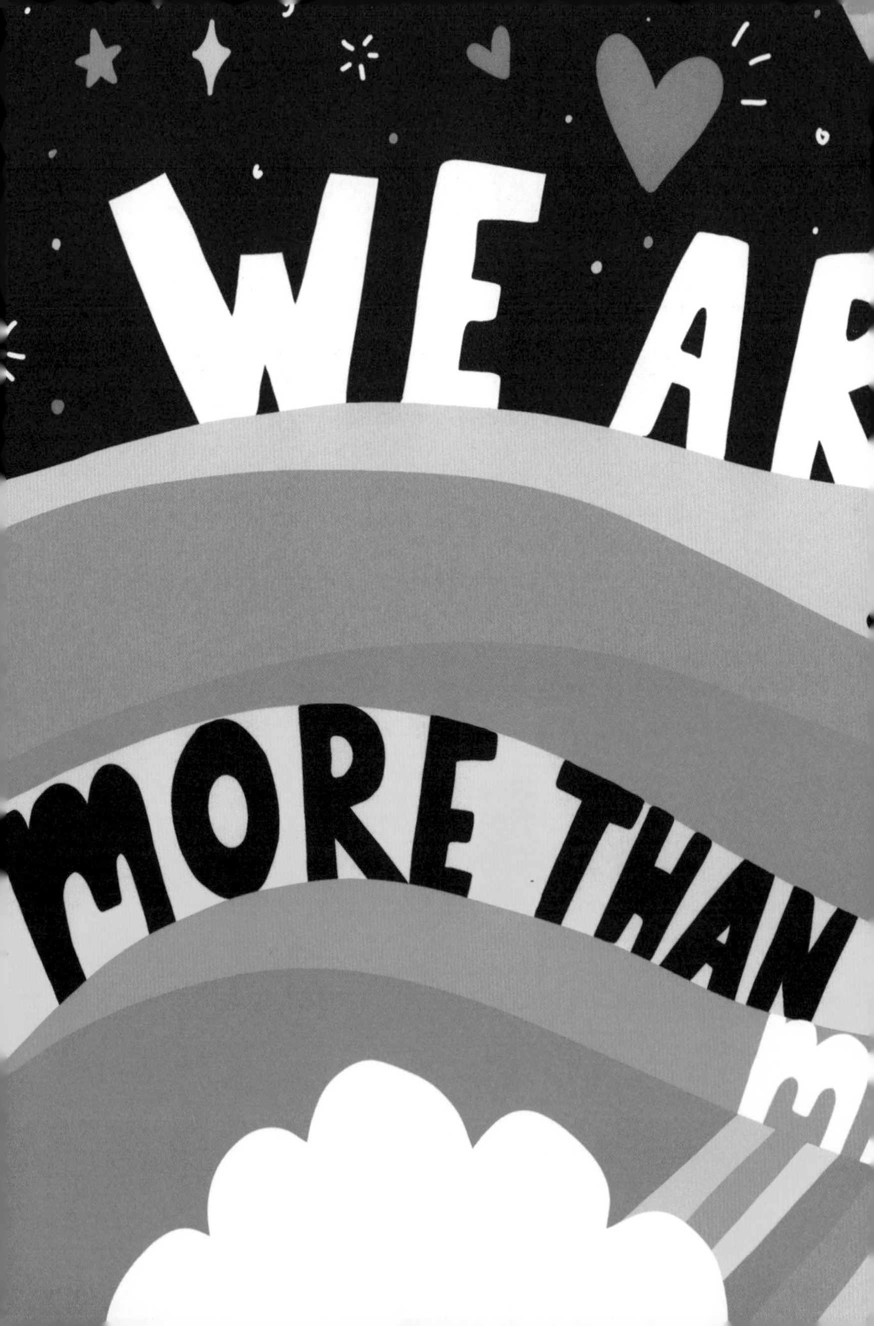
WE AR
MORE THAN

E ALL

O MUCH

ve are often

DE TO FEEL

REMIND yours:
you are when
a little CLOUD

f of who
ings get
...

P.S. you're LOVELY, KIND, BEAUTIFUL & STRONG
(IN CASE you didn't already KNOW!)

be GRATEFUL
for WHO you are
& WHAT you
DO HAVE
rather than
WHO YOU'RE NOT
& what you
DON'T HAVE.

We all have moments where we question: *'Am I enough?'*, *'Am I doing enough?'*, *'Am I clever… pretty… funny… successful enough?!'* There are many things throughout our lives that make us doubt ourselves, from constantly being told we're wrong, not feeling like you fit in or not getting good enough grades. All of these things and many more can massively knock our confidence and create doubt in almost everything we do; it's not surprising really is it?!

What if I told you: *'You are enough'*? You probably wouldn't believe me, I wouldn't either. I know that I could do more, be more, create more, read more, learn more, but we can't do all of the things all of the time. I'm realising more and more that we can't be 100% all of the time. We are constantly learning, changing, growing, reflecting – some days more than others – but right now, in this moment… you are enough, I am enough, we are enough.

I know it's much easier said than done but please try not to doubt yourself and compare yourself to others. Let's try to be grateful for who we are and what we do have rather than who we're not and what we don't have. There's so much to be grateful for; sometimes we just have to look a little harder.

friendships & Relationships

There will always be people who don't like you, no matter what you do or how hard you try, but more importantly there will ALWAYS be people who love you more than you can probably even comprehend at times. These people who feel like sunshine are the people who deserve your time and love.

NOT E

will g

yo

and that's

VERYONE
t it or

ou

solutely OK.

you ARE LOVED

Every single one of us has somebody
who loves them, no matter what.
Love is everywhere... your family and
friends you speak to every day, loved
ones you see once a year, those who
live down the road, anybody who
brings you joy... These people are
precious. Tell them you love them
as often as you can. Hug harder and
appreciate those who love you.

CONVERSATIONS can be TOUGH, saying the RIGHT thing isn't ALWAYS enough. We can't have HAPPINESS without a little PAIN. Hard times will PASS AGAIN & again.

As I've grown up (slightly) and realised that the world isn't all sunshine and rainbows all of the time, nobody's ever perfect and basically everything is a lie… just joking! I guess it can feel like that some days. One of the biggest things I've realised is that talking about stuff, whatever that stuff may be, is important and helps. I feel very fortunate to have had people in my life who I've been able to talk to; however, that doesn't mean it's always been easy to do so. A lot of the time it's been really difficult and uncomfortable and sometimes it even feels worse for having had the conversation but please don't let that put you off.

Conversations can be tough, especially when you care so much, but they also help us to share the load, let the other person/people see things from your perspective and take the weight off your shoulders.

As it can be really hard to say exactly what you want to say to somebody, whether that's your friend, parent, teacher, boss or whoever, I always find it easier writing down what I want or need to say to somebody before I say it. This allows me to process it a bit more rather than it coming out in a jumbled mess (that happens to me often).

Here are some spaces for you to write down your thoughts. You can use them for specific people or conversations you want to have or just use them as a space to scribble down whatever's on your mind... this is your book to do whatever you want with!

GO
WILD

(or not,
either
is fine!)

I just wanted to say...

35 —

please don't hold all your THOUGHTS or worries inside you x

The great thing about friends is, believe it or not, you can choose who you are friends with. *News flash!* You really don't need to be friends with people you don't like.
(I know?!)

Please don't feel pressured

As well as feeling pressure from basically every other aspect of life, relationships (both love and friendship) can come with new or unusual feelings, which are often emphasised by other changes and feelings going on inside of us, both physical and emotional. First of all, there is no 'right' time or age you should start having feelings or relationships or finding 'the one', so please do not worry or rush into something you don't feel comfortable with. Likewise, if you do start to have strong feelings, don't feel that you should shut them down 'until the time is right' or until it's too late.

After a messy teenage breakup, I vowed never to be in a relationship again. I was done with boys and the way I felt… until a few months later when a boy who had become an amazing friend, who made me laugh like nobody else, asked me to go out with him. I had just turned 17 and 10 years later, through all the ups and downs of life, we got flippin' married!

I can only speak from personal experience and I know every person is different, but at 16 years old, in those short few months of feeling like my whole world had fallen apart and my broken heart would never be fixed, I realised what was important and what I wanted or, more importantly, what I didn't want from a relationship.

What are the most important things you look for in the people you have around you?

mine: make me laugh, supportive both emotionally and physically, allow me to be me!

Social media

NOTI

THAT A

you

STUFF

FECTS

SITIVELY!

(as well as NEGATIVELY)

We're often COMPARING our own lives to an unrealistic & UNACHIEVABLE GOAL of what OUR LIVES SHOULD LOOK LIKE

Social media has become such a huge part of our lives. Most of us open and scroll through social media before anything else in the morning and often last thing at night too! I love social media, for its connections, platform to share ideas and photos and to talk to like-minded people, but sometimes it can feel like the most overwhelming place, as though everyone is shouting into a room and if you don't shout loud enough you're probably not going to be heard, not to mention the bullying, trolls, hurtful comments and judging that goes on. A big part of finding out more about why I love social media was to start actually thinking about who I was following, why I was following them and also what I was posting about myself and why.

In the same way that you don't need to be friends with people you don't like or who bring you down, you have full control over how you use social media. There can be a lot of realness, cheerleading, inspiration and love on social media if you look for it. I once saw something that described Instagram as a magazine...

Imagine you have control over what goes in that magazine you read first thing in the morning and last thing at night...

what do you want to see?

treat **Instagram** ♥ 💬 like it's a MAGAZINE you ACTUALLY WANT to FLICK through.

49

PUT YOUR PHONE DOWN

I'm not expecting you to throw your phone out of the window or even set strict times you can look at your phone (although setting yourself time limits isn't such a bad thing). The truth is, almost all of us use our phones every day and I think lots of us would agree we probably could use them less. It's more about being mindful of what we're using our phones for as well as how long we're spending on them. There's A LOT we can do instead of staring at our phones; some of my favourite things are:

- Catching up with friends face-to-face
- Going for a walk to get some fresh air
- Doing some yoga in my living room
- Baking (& eating too much of the mixture)
- Reading a book (I'm not so great at this one, I'm trying to get better)

Write down or doodle some of YOUR favourite non-phone-related things that you love doing... and try to do them every now and then!

Seeking VALIDATION from people on social media (or even in real life) ISN'T going to make you HAPPY!

fave accounts

When we are on social media, it's important we're following those who make us smile, make us feel inspired or motivated rather than constantly making us feel like we're not good enough, sad or like we're missing out. Some of my favourite insta accounts are: @i_weigh @theinsecuregirlsclub @thehappynewspaper

Can you find some positive people/ accounts to follow on social media?

♥

♥

♥

♥

♥

please look out for others

Now more than ever it is often difficult to distinguish fake from reality, which can cause such damaging effects. Just because a person is sharing lots of happy photos or responding to trolls, it doesn't mean that that person is necessarily okay. In this weird social media world we're in, where we're less likely to see our friends and families in 'real life', catching up with them through a screen instead of over a hot chocolate, it's important we try to be aware of how others might really be feeling especially when we don't know the full story. The fact that bullies and trolls can hide behind a screen allows them to treat people however they like, but as more and more of us are now realising, those negative comments can have lasting effects far bigger than you may realise, so we must look out for each other.

a few THINGS you can do:

* Check in with your loved ones in 'real life'.

* Ask people how they're doing, GENUINELY. We <u>all</u> have struggles and we ALL deal with things differently. You may not know the RIGHT thing to say but you can reach out and listen if nothing else.

* If you see somebody receiving hate or NEGATIVE comments online, send them a message, support them and ask if there's ANYTHING you can do.

* REPORT bullying online.

* Be kind, online and in 'real life', as you've no idea what people are going through.

* Think twice before you say something hurtful to somebody online. Would you <u>really</u> say that to somebody face-to-face? If not, PLEASE don't post it. Those behind a screen are real people with FEELINGS.

* Comment something POSITIVE on your friend's photos/posts online.

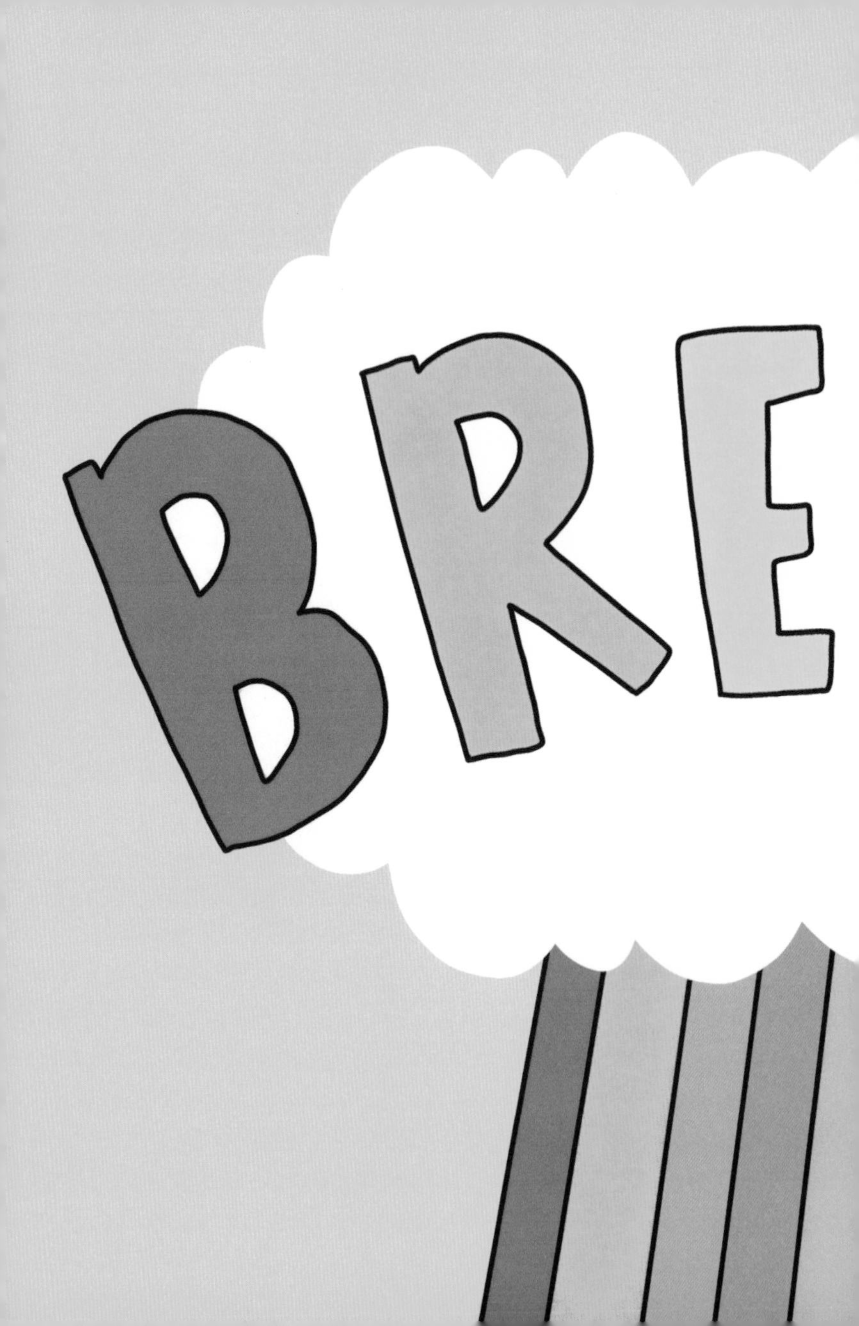
BRE

loving
yourself
♡

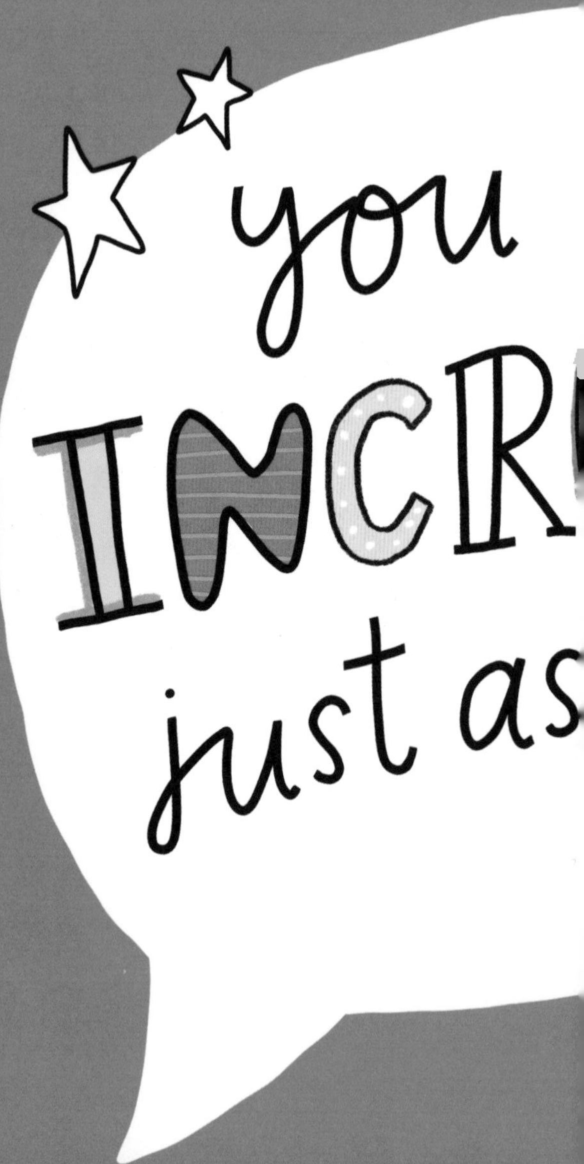
you
INCR
just as

RE

DIBLE

you are

let's TALK about
IMPERFECTIONS

With certain programmes on our TVs as well as the constant battle we all seem to have with ourselves and others, I thought this would be a good time to remind you that what you see in most TV programmes, films, magazines and a lot of what you see on social media is, quite simply, **not real**. We are constantly told that we should look and be a certain way or if we had the latest gadget or make-up we could achieve 'perfection', but at the end of the day, these are just brands and companies wanting us to buy stuff, because no brand or company (or not many at least!) is going to say, '*you know what, you are absolutely incredible just as you are... please don't change. Your imperfections are what makes you, you and that's the most magic thing*'. Other people and places might not say this to you, but I will because it's **true**.

We are taught from very early on to conform and to find flaws in ourselves – loving yourself as you are is truly a rebellious act.

being
DIFFERENT
is a GOOD THING,
BEING
YOU
is an even better THING.

In recent years I have started to accept and even embrace certain things about me that have previously really bothered me, or people have teased me for. I had a brace in high school because my front teeth really stuck out and I hated them, but those teeth are probably the most recognisable thing about me these days (in a good way!). I have often felt like I didn't quite fit in or that I was a little bit different, but trust me, being different is a good thing, and being you is an even better thing.

Please don't try to conform to an image or idea of what you think you should look or be like. Most of what you see has been Photoshopped and airbrushed or it's taken 40 selfies to get to it… Absolutely all of us have insecurities and stuff we don't like about ourselves. I have only JUST learnt to accept my stretch marks, cellulite and the little birthmark I have on my face, because I've realised that they're a part of what makes me, me, as well as the fact that I'm a real person who has grown, had experiences and moments in my life that have shaped (quite literally) the person I am today.

67

Birthmark
on my
FACE

What
are
yours?

X
X
X
X
X

Please REME

body is a **RE**

of you

everyone has a d

have LOST weight, g

have had an OPERA

due to illness... **ALL**

MAKE US

We should NEVER try

SHOULDN'T BE A

BER that your

LECTION

your life

erent story : you may

d weight, you may

ON or lifestyle change

f these THINGS

O WE ARE.

de them & DEFINITELY

AMED of them.

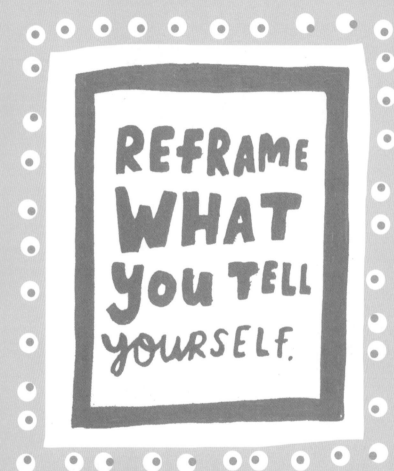

REFRAME WHAT YOU TELL YOURSELF.

Think about the way you talk to your friends, the compliments you give and even the thoughts you have. Now think about how that little voice in your brain talks to yourself.

I love your smile!

LOVIN

LITT

of

Here's to...

what do you WEIGH!?

There is an amazing initiative, which was set up on Instagram, called @I_weigh, and the basic premise is that we shouldn't measure ourselves based on how much we physically weigh. Instead, we should celebrate all the amazing things about us, our achievements, what we're grateful for, things that make us who we are, not just a number on a set of scales.

P.s. please get rid of those scales

NOW write down yours...

My WISH for you
is that you FIND
HAPPINESS
IN yourSELF
BEFORE ANYTHING or ANYONE else,
THAT you realise your
WORTH and HOW
NECESSARY
you are on
this earth.

Aside from the fact that you are a strong, independent person reading this book (yes, you!) we can still often have this overriding thought that if we find the right person then it will solve all of our problems and make us happy. The old 'happily ever after' we were all promised from a very young age probably has something to do with it.

It is so important for both you and any current or future relationship that you are able to find happiness in yourself first and learn to love and understand yourself, as best as you can! The right person loves you for all of it, the good, the bad and the 'ugly'. Likewise, try not to lose or forget yourself – it can be easy to allow a relationship to become you, but it's so important that you are still, well, you! And you have your own thing(s) too, whether that be hobbies, friends, classes or even films and TV programmes. Any sort of relationship should be a positive addition to you, and should bring out the best in both of you.

Looking after yourself

REMEMB

=yourse

and **CAR**

to SO n

ER to **GIVE**
the TIME
you give
ANY others

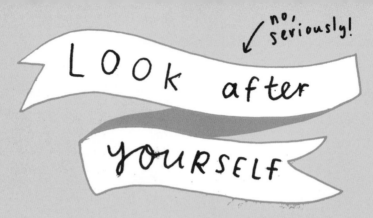

LOOK after yourself

no, seriously!

We often see or hear the term 'self-care'; it simply means taking care of ourselves. Self-care can mean different things to different people and it may change depending on how we're feeling or what we're going through, from having a relaxing bath or getting enough sleep to spending time with those you love.

Self-care isn't a handbook of what you should do – it's stuff that is going to help you personally in some way, shape or form, and it'll be different for everybody. Whatever it is that you call self-care, please make it a priority, because so many of us don't, and it can be easy to forget what counts as 'self-care'. Here are some examples:

emotional

Being aware of yourself and the things that affect you and your emotions. Check in with your emotions, identify the triggers/ things that cause you stress and focus on ways of working through and accepting them rather than hiding them away.

(let's get) physical

It may seem like an obvious thing but it can be easy to forget when we're hunched over a desk or our phones. Keep moving, stretch, walk, try yoga, swim, find an exercise class or routine that works for you... but also remember when to rest and get enough sleep too!

Social

Even if you love alone time, those around you are hugely important to your wellbeing. Notice the effect those closest to you have on your mood and inner thoughts. Keep people close to you who are loving and supportive and of course make you laugh! That's always important.

Psychological

Basically, anything that keeps your brain ticking. Learning new things, even a new skill, would be up there in this category! Practicing mindfulness, meditating and being creative, colouring, writing etc. can all help us process our thoughts and feelings.

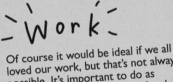

Work

Of course it would be ideal if we all loved our work, but that's not always possible. It's important to do as best as we can by making it a lovely place to work, setting boundaries, managing time and taking regular breaks.

Spiritual

This will vary for everyone (as they all will). For some 'spiritual' will include religion; for others it might be spending time in nature, charity work, meditating or just taking a few long, deep breaths. These are the things that are good for the soul.

self-care is:

HOT CHOCOLATE & BISCUITS
FAVE SONGS
DRINKING WATER
washing bedding
NOT STARING at a screen
Getting ENOUGH SLEEP
PAINTING NAILS
FRESH AIR!
petting DOGS!
tidying /organising stuff
bubble bath
Watching a SUNSET

what does SELF-CARE mean to you?

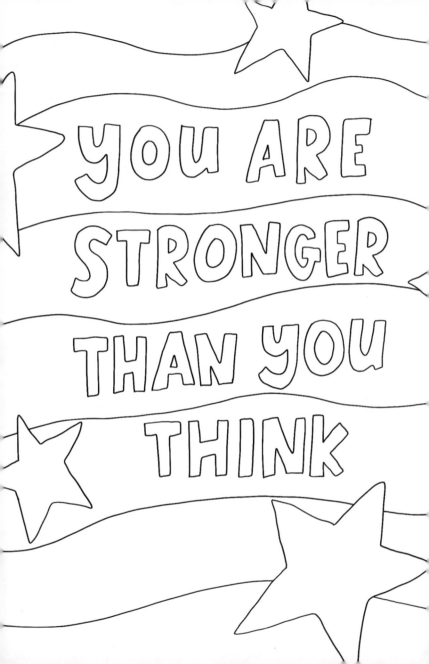

STUFF to do
WHEN YOU'RE FEELING OVERWHELMED

GET SOME FRESH AIR

Have a little NAP!

TALK to SOMEBODY

WRITE THINGS DOWN

what are your favourite THINGS to do when you're OVERWHELMED?

your mental HEALTH

IF YOU'RE
YOU HAVE S
WHOLE LIF
VERY mom
IT THROUGH YOUR
EXPERIENCED HEAR
LOVE AND HAPPINE
and KNOW YOU'RE
LOOK at you GO! WHA

EADING THIS
RVIVED YOUR
UP UNTIL THIS
T. YOU'VE MADE

ARKEST DAYS. YOU'VE
REAK AND SADNESS,
TAKE A DEEP BREATH
NG a SUPERB JOB!
a SUPERSTAR.

PLEASE TALK or go for a walk

KNOW that it's OKAY TO BE SAD

please DON'T feel BAD

ASK for SUPPORT

LAUGH UNTIL YOU SNORT

write, PAINT & draw

be SILLY on the dance floor

TAKE BREAKS EAT CAKES

appreciate lovely things

& embrace all that life brings

LOOKING after ourselves & our whirling brains

I'm sure you've heard a lot about mental health; it's only in recent years that I have actually begun to understand it more and be able to talk openly about it. I certainly don't know everything there is to know, and mental health is very different for each person, but the biggest thing I have learnt, and try to reiterate as much as possible, is that mental health is as important as, if not more so than, physical health.

See, we all have mental health in the same way we all have physical health. We all get sickness bugs and colds in the same way as we've all had some level of stress, anxiety or mental health struggle. Our symptoms might not be the same as the next person but that's because our minds are incredibly complex things, something we probably won't ever fully understand, which can make mental health much harder to deal with.

We all must take care of our own mental health. One thing I want you to know is that it's okay to be sad. It's okay not to be able to explain how you feel; you don't owe anybody an explanation. It's okay to feel confused, angry or emotional and not really know why. Recognising how you feel is important, and talking to somebody about it, or even writing your thoughts down, is the biggest step you'll take to understanding your struggles more, and therefore being able to receive help or support from a friend, loved one or a professional.

If you're struggling and would like to talk to somebody about how you're feeling, I have popped a list of contacts in the back of this book (page 175).

YOUR MENTAL HEALTH IS A PRIORITY

how are you FEELING?

If you don't fancy writing down how you feel you might rather fill out your expression/mood on different days instead:

everything is OKAY

things that are okay today...
* MY HAIR! REALLY
  * (this is ACTUALLY hard to do)
* MY WARDROBE (my clothes)
* MY WEIGHT/BODY (took me a whi
* FAMILY & FRIENDS ❤   to realis
  this)
* MY HEALTH ↑   ← ok, it's getti
  easier!
  & theirs!!

Now your turn...

FIND who
you are

HO YOU
OT WHO
HINK YOU
OULD BE

Staying TRUE to yourself is IMPORTANT

I think all of us, at some point, have that inner critic in our brains constantly making us question our every choice and action: *'What if they don't like me?' 'What if that was a stupid thing to say?' 'What if they're judging me?' 'What if nobody likes my thoughts/ideas/ work/passion?!'* I have had SO many of these thoughts throughout my life, even writing this book, I have no idea if anybody will like or appreciate it (I really hope you do, oh my!). I try to be honest and open about my thoughts and feelings; I'm very much a 'what you see is what you get' kinda girl, and I try to remind myself that nobody will be liked or appreciated by absolutely everybody. The world would be a very boring place if we were all exactly the same.

We will never fully know what everybody thinks of us, and I'm pretty sure we wouldn't want to know, but staying true to yourself is important. Don't lose sight of your opinions, thoughts and feelings amongst the whirlwind of everybody else's.

I'm often that person in a group (one I'm not fully comfortable with) who will stay quiet and listen to everybody else's opinion and my brain will be going *'BUT YOU DON'T AGREE WITH THAT, TELL THEM ABOUT THAT TIME YOU EXPERIENCED IT FIRST HAND'* etc.

I think we can worry so much about sounding stupid or being judged that we stay silent at times, and I want to let you know that it is uncomfortable and *really* difficult at times to put yourself out there, especially if we think those around us are far more eloquent with their words or know more about x, y and z. But, I'll be the first to hold my hand up and say this is basically how I feel every time I say anything! When we believe in something strongly we can risk being defensive the moment it's knocked or challenged, but that's life. We all naturally want to be liked and accepted, but we also all make mistakes and can't always get everything right. It's absolutely okay to admit that.

WRITE DOWN your inner critic THOUGHTs...

YOU'RE NOT clever ENOUGH

Now I'm not saying you should go on a mission and out of your way to stand out, but I am saying you don't need to worry about fitting in by looking or acting like anyone else; you are unique, so don't ever forget that. If you feel comfortable, confident or happy in something, don't you dare think that anyone else should have a say in how it looks. The truth is not everybody is going to like what you wear or how you style your hair (or whatever else) but it doesn't matter as long as you feel happy.

If we all dressed, acted and looked the same it would be the most boring place ever, so please find that pair of rainbow trousers or fluffy jumper that makes you feel like nobody else's opinion matters. Trust me, it's such a great feeling when you let go of that need for acceptance, and it can have such a positive impact on yourself and those around you too.

Please UNDERSTAND that when somebody says NASTY or hurtful COMMENTs... it says far more about them than it does about you.

WHAT'S *your* STORY?

I know this is probably a really obvious, clichéd thing that you've been told on more than one occasion, but I think it's important to reiterate it because it can be easy to forget when we receive hurtful comments, whether online or in real life. People who say nasty things, those who want to put others down for absolutely any reason, are doing so because of their own issues or insecurities. We have no idea what other people have been through or what their story is, and it is sometimes easier for people to project their own problems, issues or even things that have been said to them on to others, which can result in you or me getting the brunt of it. The sooner you can realise and accept this, the *slightly* easier it is to understand where those hurtful comments are coming from and know they are *not* a reflection of you.

Dear younger Em,

Never stop laughing! You might get sent out of
class for laughing at times, but you'll realise
that most teachers and classmates will comment
on your infectious smile and laugh more than
anything else. You'll even win the 'Biggest Grin'
when you leave school in a few months. I wish
I could tell tiny Em that her worst feature,
her 'big teeth', will end up being her favourite
(you grow into them!). Your smile may also play
a teeny tiny part in you setting up your own
business (oh yeah, by the way, you set up your
own business 6 years from now?!). Whaat!?

Happiness is more important than any grade
you could get, but do keep working hard to
achieve the best you can (they won't be that
important, but I know you wouldn't have it any
other way). At each stage of education you'll
feel like you're being held back, but ohh boy do
you prove them wrong. I think the doubt from
others actually strengthens your determination,
so just keep doing you... It's such a cliché but
hard work really does pay off. Please remember
to rest and have some 'me time' as often as you
need though. Spoiler alert: you need it often!
Focus on the stuff you're passionate about, keep

drawing, writing and taking photos... you are going to have the BEST opportunities with all of these (I won't ruin the surprises...). he he

I could warn you about all the good and bad things that are going to happen, as there will be a whole bunch, but you need to experience all of these to shape the person you are now, writing this letter, and the person you're going to become. Surround yourself with good people... those who bring out the best in you but please know that not everybody stays in your life and although hard to comprehend, it's sometimes necessary.

You'll be told you're different... that's definitely a good thing. Don't try to fit in — you'll realise that for yourself. Your broken heart will be fixed, it takes a little while but it's important, you just trust me on this one. You might not realise it or be bothered right now... but you are SO loved; whenever you feel a little lost you must remember that and remind those you love as often as you can too. Stay true to yourself and hold on to that childlike sense of wonder and adventure — we could all do with a bit more of that every now and then.

Lots and lots of love from slightly older you x

WRITE a letter to your younger self...

KINDNESS

IN a
where
ANY
BE I

NORLD
ou can be
HING,
IND.

One of the first things you probably think about when you hear the word 'kindness' is compliments – hopefully a few compliments you've received in the past will spring to mind. Although being told you look gorgeous or have lovely hair is wonderful, let's have a think about some *non-appearance-related compliments* we could give to those we know or interact with on a daily basis...

* The world (my world) is a better place having you in it

* you're so kind ♥

* I LOVE your outlook on life

* you're one of the strongest/bravest people I know

* your laugh is the <u>BEST</u>

* you make others feel good!

think of some more
(non-appearance-related)
compliments maybe
you've received...

DON'T FORGET to REFLECT ON THE POSITIVES

PEOPLE WILL ALWAYS FIND NEGATIVES

One thing we must realise is that people will ALWAYS find negatives in anything you do, say, look, dress or speak (the list goes on!). In a world that is so quick to tear us apart and bring us down. We can make a change by being kind, celebrating the positives and lifting each other up. We need so much more of that.

FIND the POSITIVES

Think of some positive things that have happened this week...

my FRIEND PASSED her EXAMS!

FIND POSITIVES IN THE EVERY-DAY

everybod.
or meet is
stuff you
about. We're
own battles e

you See
ing through
ave no idea
l fighting our
ery Single day

BE MINDFUL about what you consume DAILY

You may feel like you're fully aware of the messages you consume on a daily basis, and it can't have THAT much of an effect anyway... can it? It can be helpful to take note of things throughout your day that have a positive or negative effect on you i.e. scrolling through social media, seeing the news, the food we see advertised etc.

focus on the GOOD

I set up *The Happy Newspaper* when I realised the impact negative news was having on my mental health and that of many people around me. The aim isn't to pretend that terrible things don't happen, because of course they do; the idea is that I think we deserve to have the good stuff recognised and celebrated, rather than be bombarded with a constant stream of all the bad stuff happening in the world. When we share positive stories it inspires us to do good too. See if you can find any positive stories...

HAPPY NEWS

a LOVELY NEWS story

HAPPY FACT:

an ACT OF KINDNESS I WITNESSED:

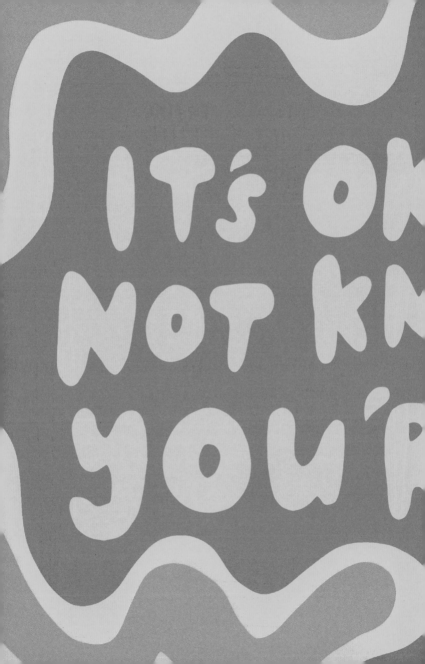

look at you GROW

LOOK at you GROW

You have come so far! You might not realise it every day, but think about where you were a year ago... or five years ago! Just think about how much you have accomplished, how much you've been through and now you're stronger than ever. You are constantly growing, and we often forget to stop for a minute and reflect back on all the amazing stuff, as well as the not so great stuff. All of it matters, all of it makes us who we are and it shouldn't be taken for granted.

ONE DAY YOU WILL LOOK BACK ON THIS MOMENT AND REALISE HOW MUCH YOU'VE GROWN.

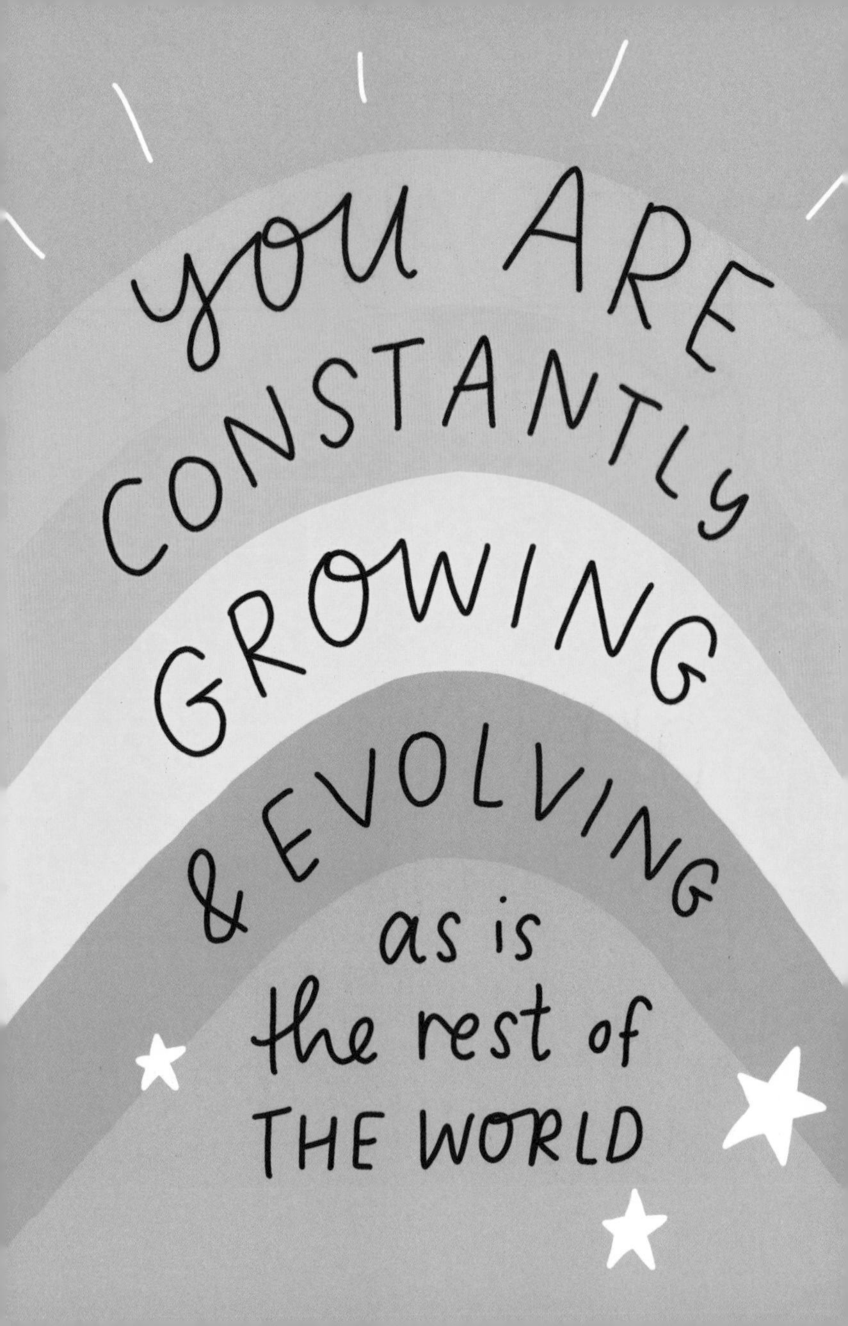
YOU ARE
CONSTANTLY
GROWING
& EVOLVING
as is
the rest of
THE WORLD

As we grow and evolve it's important we try to be as self-aware as possible, which is a lot easier said than done sometimes! It means focusing on ourselves but also understanding that the world and the people in it are also changing and evolving around us, which can sometimes be confusing or stressful. There is always room for growth and change, but this can also come with uncertainty, as most of us, on the surface, would quite like things to just tick along as they are. We can all make more positive choices or changes and you're never too old to learn something new or make a change.

THINGS I want to do / LEARN / CHANGE

We're constantly made to feel like we could be better versions of ourselves and the aim of this book is to take away those pressures and remind you just how incredible you are. However, almost all of us have things we'd like to change, do more/less of and maybe even something new we'd like to learn! There is a difference between being stuck in your ways and not changing anything about you or your life, and learning, adapting and growing as we all do every single day.

These could be tiny things: I'd like to do more reading, spend less time scrolling through my phone, and learning the best cookie recipe definitely improved my life! It isn't about massive life changes or spending loads of time or money on stuff that's going to 'make our lives better'; it's small steps we can all take to improve our day-to-day lives and the lives of those around us too.

Something I could do more of...

Something I could CHANGE...

Something I want to learn...

Something I could do less of...

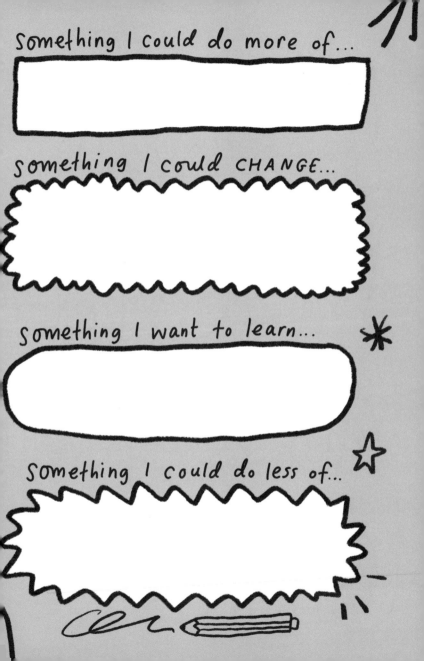

PLEAS

WORL

ABOUT TH

CAN'T

STOP
YING
NGS YOU
CONTROL

What DO I have control over?

We spend so much time worrying about stuff we can't control, it's good to remind ourselves of what we DO have control over. I've given you a few examples; see if you can think of any more...

* Who you're FRIENDS with
* How often you say thank you
*
*
*
*
*

What do I NOT
have control over...

* The way people ACT and behave

* what other people think of you

*

*

*

*

*

FAILING IS OKAY & NECESSARY.

Failing is normal. Some of the biggest, most famous and successful people in the world have been 'failures' – honestly, google it! We are taught very early on in our life that failing is bad and wrong, but it is a hugely important part of any learning process. Failing at something allows us to reflect and move forward. You can learn so much from mistakes and failure; remember that these things do not define you, they teach you things about yourself that you probably didn't even realise before.

learn from FAILURE

WHAT WENT RIGHT?

HOW DID YOU FEEL?

HAT HAVE YOU LEARNED?

WHAT COULD YOU DO DIFFERENT NEXT TIME?

IT'S
about
BALA

(WHATEVER the HELL THAT IS)

SEE HOW FAR YOU'VE COME

Don't forget to celebrate the small and massive stuff. Writing these things down can be such a wonderful and important reminder when we feel stuck or uninspired.

SOME stuff I've achieved...

woop woop!

dreams
REALLY
DO COME TRUE!

What are
YOUR
dreams?

WRITE
them
DOWN...

DO YO

and KNOW

your BES

DIFFERENT t

R BEST

that doing

T will mean

gs on DIFFERENT days.

THE
FUTURE

Go for it and go for it Passionately

If you have a thought or idea, go for it! Often we put stuff off so much because we're not sure, we don't have the time or we don't even fully know what 'it' is. Often people ask me when they should start their *insert dream/ambition/goal/passion/business here* and the answer is NOW. It might not work, it might take a few years to become a thing or for you to realise whether you love or hate it, but start with the basics... Do some research, read a book, write a list or save a little bit of money. If you're passionate enough about something, you can do it, but you must be prepared to work really, really hard at it. We see so many things happen 'instantly' these days, but more often than not they have taken months, if not years, of hard work, dedication, passion and probably a few tears and meltdowns along the way.

Where to start...

what is it?

MAKE a to-do LIST:

FIND SOME BOOKS:

WHY DO you WANT TO DO 'THE thing':

I like to think we all have a BRIGHT LIGHT inside of us & at different moments throughout our lives, that LIGHT is going to SHINE SO BRIGHTLY. But that light shouldn't be compared with others. We will need other people's bright lights in dark or FOGGY times, in the SAME way that people will need ours too. And that's the BEAUTY of this FUNNY thing we call life... Not everybody's LIGHTs are going to be SHINING BRIGHTLY at the same time.

the little
THINGs count

This funny thing we call life can be an amazing and magical thing and then it can be crappy and then it can be wonderful again. We will experience the highest highs and the lowest lows and in between the extremes will be pretty normal, everyday stuff... On some (most) days those little things will be the things that matter... We might not remember them for years to come, we might not celebrate them or even really acknowledge them, but the little things – like leaving someone a handwritten note, calling your grandparents or dipping your toes in the ocean – really do count.

the
future
IS BRIGHT
AND SPARKLY
& OTHER LOVELY
THINGS but also
will be a bit TOUGH
at times & that's ok too.

UNCERTAINTY

When we look to the future, for some of us it's super-exciting and for others it fills us with dread and uncertainty. Both are totally normal, and we can even feel all of those feelings at the same time.

Nobody knows what the future holds, but what we do know is that there will be a whole heap of good and bad stuff along the way. There will be amazing moments you cannot even comprehend right now. You will meet wonderful people who get 'it' – and you! There will also be times in your life when you can't see a way out, things that will throw you off course completely out of the blue. Give yourself time to process both the good and the bad; we can be so focused on 'finding the positives' that we don't give ourselves time to process the messy stuff.

STRETCH

DRINK MORE WAT

TURN the MUSIC
(or down)
PUT YO

TAKE A DEEP
BREATH

DANCE in the KITCHE

look UP at the STARS

OP THE KETTLE ON

put YOUR
COMFY PANTS ON

PHONE DOWN FOR A BIT

AINT even if you haven't before

PLASH IN A PUDDLE

ear your favourite outfit

EE HOW MANY DOGS YOU CAN PET...

ee how many smiles you GET!

REMEMBE

YOU FE

THERE WII

WHEN Y

HAPPY

... WHENEVER

EL SAD,

BE A TIME

U FEEL

AGAIN

Thank you so much **to you** for reading and scribbling in this book. I hope it's like a little colourful burst of joy every time you pick it up. Thank you to my editors Sam and Emma for basically allowing me to create it and share my words and doodles – you're magic. Thank you to my family and friends who are constant cheerleaders and have unknowingly taught me a lot of the stuff in this book. Thank you to Niall for supporting me always, and for being a constant reminder that love is real, and kindness and laughter are the most important things in life.

If you need somebody to talk to about your own mental health, please seek the advice and support of your GP.

Below are the details of other services and organisations who can offer help and support:

SAMARITANS: 116 123 / www.samaritans.org

RETHINK MENTAL ILLNESS: For practical advice on therapy, medication, money and your rights under the Mental Health Act 0300 5000 927

PAPYRUS: Prevention of Young Suicide 0800 068 41 41 / www.papyrus-uk.org

MIND: 0300 123 3393 / www.mind.org.uk

SANE: 0300 304 7000 / www.sane.org.uk

BEFRIENDERS: www.befrienders.org For support outside the UK

YOUNGMINDS: 020 7089 5050 / www.youngminds.org.uk

3 5 7 9 10 8 6 4 2

Vermilion, an imprint of Ebury Publishing,
20 Vauxhall Bridge Road,
London, SW1V 2SA

Vermilion is part of the Penguin Random House group
of companies whose addresses can be found at global.
penguinrandomhouse.com

Penguin
Random House
UK

First published by Vermilion in 2020

www.penguin.co.uk

A CIP catalogue record for this book is available from the British
Library

Design: Emily Coxhead

ISBN: 9781785043154

Printed and bound in Italy by Printer Trento S.r.l.

Penguin Random House is committed to a sustainable future for
our business, our readers and our planet. This book is made from
Forest Stewardship Council® certified paper.